THINGS I DIDN'T KNOW I LOVED

Selected
Poems of
Nazim Hikmet

Translated by

Randy Blasing & Mutlu Konuk

Things I Didn't Know I Loved

 Persea Books, Inc.

Copyright © 1975 by Randy Blasing and Mutlu Konuk
Published simultaneously in Canada by
    McGraw-Hill Ryerson Ltd.
All rights reserved.

For information, address the publisher:
    Persea Books, Inc.
    Box 804 Madison Square Station
    New York, N.Y. 10010
International Standard Book Number: 0-89255-000-7, cloth
                                    0-89255-001-5, paper
Library of Congress Catalog Card Number: 75-10789
First Printing
Printed in the United States of America

CONTENTS

Nazim Hikmet, the first and greatest modern Turkish poet, has not been widely translated in the United States, yet his work is well known throughout the rest of the world, where he is regarded as one of the great international poets of the twentieth century. Hikmet was born in 1902 in Salonika, which was then part of the Ottoman Empire, and grew up in Istanbul. His mother was a painter, and his grandfather a "gentleman poet"; through their circle of friends he was introduced to poetry early, publishing his first poems at seventeen. Following the First World War, he left Allied-occupied Istanbul to teach in Eastern Turkey. Attracted by what was happening in Russia, however, he shortly made his way up to Tiflis and eventually arrived in Moscow in the heady days of 1922. During the next two years he studied economics and political science at the university and met poets and artists from all over the world. He returned to Turkey after the Turkish Independence and worked for a leftist magazine in Istanbul. When the staff of the magazine was arrested, Hikmet—who was in Izmir running an underground press at the time—was sentenced to fifteen years. His novel *It's Great to Be Alive, My Friend* records his experience of hiding out in Izmir before he was able to escape to Russia in 1926. Back in Moscow, he met Mayakovsky, worked with Meyerhold, and wrote plays until 1928, when he could return to Turkey after a general amnesty. By this time, however, the Turkish government had outlawed the Communist Party and was moving more and more to the right, and Hikmet was arrested upon his return. Although he was subsequently released for lack of "evidence," this adventure was a taste of things to come, for throughout the thirties he was in and out of prison for being a Marxist.

His first book, *835 Lines*, was published in Istanbul in 1929, and his first long poem, *Gioconda and Si-Ya-U*, appeared later the same year. Funny, fresh, and audacious, these early poems created a great deal of excitement among younger Turkish writers and announced Hikmet's arrival as a new, major poet. A second collection, *3 Coming Up*, and a collaboration, *1 + 1 = One*, came out the next year, and *The City That Lost Its Voice*, which contained Hikmet's "replies" to hostile members of the reactionary literary establishment, followed in 1931. Hikmet went on to publish *Night Telegram* (1932) and *Why Banerjee Killed Himself* (1933), another long poem which was an attack not only on imperialism but on the bourgeois concept of life and art. Subsequently, he was arrested in a general roundup of radicals on the grounds that his books were being read by workers. Although none of his books had been condemned at this time, he was sentenced to five years but served only one and a half. Like all suspected Communists during the thirties, Hikmet was under constant surveillance by the Turkish secret police. Since his books continued to sell, however, publishers kept taking them on, but in order to make a living Hikmet worked as a proofreader, translator, and scriptwriter. In 1935 the appearance of *Letters to Taranta-Babu*, a response to Mussolini in North Africa, forced Hikmet to go underground and to publish his political newspaper articles under a pseudonym. During the same year he published another book of poetry, *Portraits*, and a play, *The Forgotten Man. The Epic of Sheik Bedreddin*, an important long poem inspired by Hikmet's reading about a fourteenth-century Turkish peasants' revolt, came out in 1936 and was his last book to be published in Turkey during his lifetime.

In January 1938, Hikmet was arrested on the charge of inciting military cadets to revolt. On the evidence that the cadets read and admired his poetry, military courts sentenced him to a total of thirty-five years. This sentence was subsequently reduced to twenty-eight years, and Hikmet went to prison for the last time. During his imprisonment he conceived of and began work on his mammoth epic, *Human Landscapes from My Country*; however, since some of the people entrusted with parts of the manuscript chose to destroy them for fear of prosecution, and because other parts fell into the hands of the police, it appears that only 17,000 lines of the original poem have survived. In prison he also met—and, in some cases, helped to educate—many important writers and artists, for in these years prisons were the center of Turkish intellectual life. In 1949, however, a world-wide committee—which included Eluard, Aragon, Sartre, Picasso, Neruda, and Robeson—was founded in Paris to rescue Hikmet from prison, and in 1950 Hikmet himself went on an eighteen-day hunger strike, despite having just suffered a heart attack. He also received the World Peace Prize the same year. After all this, he was finally released in a general amnesty in 1950. Thus, of the twenty-two years that Hikmet lived in Turkey after his return from Russia in 1928, seventeen were spent in prison.

After his release, Hikmet lived in Turkey with his third wife for less than a year before the anti-Communist Turkish government came up with the solution of drafting him. Forced to leave his family behind, he fled Turkey in a small fishing boat; he was rescued by a Romanian ship in the Black Sea and arrived in Moscow in 1951. During his exile Hikmet lived in Moscow, Bulgaria, Warsaw, and Paris and not only traveled widely in Europe but visited Peking, Havana, and Tanganyika: "I traveled through Europe, Asia, and Africa with my dream / only the Americans didn't give me a visa." He continued to be productive during this period; indeed, his last poems—quiet, open, and always threatening to lapse into prose—represent a major rediscovery of his art. He died in Moscow in 1963.

Although a *Selected Poems* was published in Sofia in 1951, Hikmet's books began to appear in Turkey only after the U.S.-subsidized Menderes regime was overthrown in 1960. In 1965-66, for example, more than twenty books by Hikmet were published there, some of them reprints of earlier books and others works appearing for the first time. Since then a two-volume *Selected Poems* has appeared, as well as the five-book epic, *Human Landscapes from My Country*, and, most recently, *Last Poems*. At the same time, two biographies of Hikmet have been published, and his novels, plays, letters, and even children's stories have also come out. Today Hikmet is generally recognized in Turkey not only as the greatest modern poet but as one of the best poets ever to write in Turkish.

Throughout his career Hikmet conceived of his art as inseparable from his life, and in his work poetic purpose and political responsibility are one. For his poems *are* political: while he does not provide us with political commentary, he does accept that the purpose of his art is to change the world. Yet, for Hikmet, only the kind of art that changes itself can change the world. Thus Hikmet is a major Turkish poet because he brought an entirely new kind of poetry into Turkish literature, revolutionizing poetic technique, subject matter, and language. And he is a great international poet because his innovativeness as a poet is inseparable from his vision of a new life in a new world.

Perfectly alert to what is going on around him, and with the large poetic freedom of a Whitman, Hikmet writes at once of his century, his culture, and himself. For his poems are also personal, even autobiographical. He records his life, never reducing it to self-consciousness and always affirming the reality of facts. Dates, for example, are very important for Hikmet; indeed, the date of a poem often becomes part of the poem itself. It is the conjunction of fact and feeling, however, that makes for a poetry at once public and personal, and Hikmet never doubts the validity of his feelings. What emerges from his poems, then, is his human *presence*; the strongest impression that we get from his poetry is a sense of Hikmet as a person. And it is the controlling figure of Hikmet's personality—playful, optimistic, and capable of childlike joy—that enables his poetry to remain open, public, and committed to change without ever becoming programmatic.

In the perfect oneness of his life and art, Hikmet stands as a heroic figure. In his early poems he proclaims this unity as a faith: art is an event, he insists, not only in literary history but in social history. As a result, the poet's bearing in his art is inseparable from his bearing in life. Cowardice in one is cowardice in the other; courage in one is courage in the other. The rest of Hikmet's life gave him a chance to act upon this faith and, in fact, to deepen it. In a sense, his prosecutors honored him by believing that a book of poems could incite the army to revolt; indeed, the fact that he was persecuted attests to the credibility of his faith in the vital importance of his art. Yet the suffering that his faith cost him—he never compromised in his life or art—is only secondary to the suffering that must have gone into maintaining that faith. For poetry, as Hikmet writes, is "the bloodiest of the arts"—one must offer his heart to others and feed on it himself. Thus the circumstances of Hikmet's life are very much to the point, not only because he continually made the choice not to betray his vision, but because his life and art have a dramatic completeness. Sartre has written that Hikmet conceived of a human being as something to be created. And it was in his life, no less than in his art, that Hikmet forged this new human being—who was heroic because he was a *creator*. This conception of the artist as a hero and of the hero as a creator saves art from becoming a frivolous activity in the modern world; as Hikmet's career dramatizes, poetry is indeed a matter of life and death.

Mutlu Konuk

TRANSLATORS' NOTE

In making this selection we chose poems that we liked both in Turkish and in translation. At the same time, we have tried not only to represent the major "periods" of Hikmet's career but to suggest his range as a poet, for he was capable of writing many different *kinds* of poems. Moreover, since Hikmet is known as much for his epic poems as for his lyrics, any selection would be incomplete without an example of his narrative poetry. Instead of doing parts of his various long poems, we have translated his first long poem in its entirety, and it is probably the most accessible—to Western readers—of his longer works. Finally, we have attempted to remain faithful to Hikmet's usually very colloquial Turkish by staying as close to spoken American English as his meaning would permit.

Our thanks to Stephen Berg, Michael Braziller, and Meral Konuk for helping make this book possible.

R. B.
M. K.

Some of these translations originally appeared in
The American Poetry Review.

1

Early Poems

Taut thick fingers punch
the teeth of my typewriter.
Three words are down on paper,
        the letters set in capitals:
SPRING
  SPRING
    SPRING . . .
And I, poet, proofreader,
and I, the man who's forced to read
2,000 bad lines
    every day
        for two liras,
and I,
  since spring is here,
    why am I
      like a ragged
        black chair
          still sitting?
My head put on its cap by itself
    I flew out of the printer's
      I'm on the street.
The lead dirt of the composing room
            on my face,
75 kuruş in my pocket.
        SPRING IN THE AIR . . .

In barbershops
    they're powdering
      the yellow cheeks
        of the pariah of Babiâli.
And in the shop windows
    three-color bookcovers
      flash like sun-struck mirrors.
But me,
I don't have even a book of ABC's
that lives on this street

and carries my name on its door!
But what the hell . . .
I don't look back,
the lead dirt of the composing room
                    on my face,
75 kuruş in my pocket.
          SPRING IN THE AIR . . .

                    *

This writing got left in the middle.
It rained and swamped the lines.
But oh! what I was going to write . . .
The hungry writer who sits on his 3,000-page
                              3-volume manuscript
was not going to stare at the window of the *kebapçi,*
but with his shining eyes was going to take
the Armenian bookseller's dark plump daughter by storm . . .
The sea was going to start smelling sweet.
Spring was going to rear up
              like a sweating red mare,
and leaping onto its bare back
                    I'd ride
        it into the water.
Then
    my typewriter was to follow
          me every step of the way.
I'd say to it:
        "Oh, don't do it!
            Leave me alone for an hour . . ."
Then
my head—its hair falling out—
      was to shout into the distance:
          I AM IN LOVE . . .

I'm 27
she's 17.
Blind Cupid
lame Cupid
blind and lame Cupid
said, Come love this girl,

I was going to say;
I *couldn't* say,
I can *still* say!

But if
　　　it was raining,
if the lines I wrote got swamped,
if I have 25 kuruş left in my pocket,
　　　　　　　　what the hell . . .
Hey, spring is here spring is here spring
　　　　　　　　　spring is here!

My blood is budding inside me!!

20–21 April 1929

Sometimes I too tell the ah's
of my heart one by one
like the blood-red beads of a ruby rosary,
and this red-gleaming rosary
                    is strung on strands of golden hair! . . .
But
the wings that spread from the shoulders
of the muse that inspires
my
poetry are made of the iron I-beams
                    of my suspension bridges!

One can listen to it—
                    it's not that you can't listen to
the lament of the nightingale to the rose . . .
But the language
            I really understand
is Beethoven sonatas played
on copper, iron, wood, bone, and catgut . . .

You can *have*
riding your horse off
in a cloud of dust!
Me, I wouldn't trade
for even the purest-bred
            Arabian horse
the 110 kilometers-an-hour
                    of my iron horse
                    that runs on iron tracks!

Sometimes like a big dumb fly my eye is caught
by the masterly spider webs in the corner of my room . . .
But what I really look up to
are the 77-story, reinforced-concrete mountains
                    whose creators are my blue-shirted architects!

Were I to meet
the male beauty
"young Adonis, god of Biblos"
on a bridge, I'd probably pass without looking at him;
but I can't pass by without looking
into the eyes of my bespectacled philosopher
or into the square face of my fireman,
                              which burns like a sweating sun!

Although I can smoke
third-class cigarettes filled
on my electric workbenches,
I can't roll tobacco—not even Samsun—
in paper by hand and smoke it!
I didn't trade—
                    I wouldn't trade—
my wife in her leather cap and leather jacket
for Eve's nakedness!
Perhaps I lack "poetic ardor"?
What can I do!
        when more than the children of mother earth
                                          I love
                                          my own children!

                              1926

A CLAIM

To the memory of my friend SI-YA-U,
whose head was cut off in Shanghai

Renowned Leonardo's
world-famous
La Gioconda
has disappeared.
And in the space
vacated by the fugitive
a copy has been placed.

The poet inscribing
the present treatise
knows more than a little
about the fate
of the real Gioconda.
She fell in love
with a seductive
graceful boy:
a honey-tongued
almond-eyed Chinese
by the name of SI-YA-U.
Gioconda ran off
after her lover;
Gioconda got burned
in a Chinese city.

I, Nazim Hikmet,
authority
on this matter,
thumbing my nose at friend and foe
five times a day,
undaunted,
claim
I can prove it;
if I can't,
I'll be ruined and forced into exile
forever from the realm of poesy.

1928

Part One
Excerpts from Gioconda's Diary

15 March 1924 Paris, Louvre Museum

At last I am bored with the Louvre Museum.
One gets fed up with boredom very soon.
I am fed up with my boredom.
And from the ruin inside me
     I drew this lesson:
         To visit
             a museum is fine,
           to be a museum-piece is terrible!
In this palace that imprisons the past
I am placed under such a heavy sentence
that as the paint on my face cracks out of boredom
I'm forced to keep grinning without letting up.
Because:
   I am the Gioconda from Florence
whose smile is more famous than Florence.
I am bored with the Louvre Museum.
And since one gets sick soon enough
                of talking with the past,
I decided
   from now on
to keep a diary.
Writing of today may be of some help
              in forgetting yesterday . . .
However, the Louvre is a strange place.
Here you might find
Alexander the Great's
   Longines watch complete with chronometer,
but
you can't find a sheet of clean notebook paper
or a pencil worth a piaster.
Damn your Louvre, your Paris.
I'll write these entries
         on the back of my canvas.
And so

when I stole a pen from the pocket
of a nearsighted American
            sticking his red nose into my skirts—
his hair stinking of wine—
                        I started my memoirs.
I'm writing on my back
    the sorrows of having a famous smile . . .

18 March Night

The Louvre has fallen asleep.
In the darkness the armless body of the Venus
                        looks like a veteran of the Great War.
The golden helmet of a knight shines
as the light from the night watchman's lantern
                                    strikes a dark picture.
Here
        in the Louvre
                    my days are all the same
                        like the four sides of a wooden cube.
My head is full of sharp smells
            like the shelf of a medicine cabinet.

20 March

I admire those Flemish painters:
Is it easy to give the air of a naked goddess
                                    to the plump ladies
of milk and sausage merchants?
However,
    even if one wears silk pants,
cow + silk pants = cow.

Last night
    a window
        was left open.
The naked Flemish goddesses caught cold.
All day
today,

turning their bare
mountainlike pink behinds to the public,
                              they coughed and sneezed . . .
I too caught cold.
So as not to look silly smiling with a cold,
I tried to hide my sniffles
                    from the visitors.

1 April

Today I saw a Chinese:
        he was nothing like those Chinese with their lovelocks.
How long
      he gazed at me!
I'm well aware
      that the favor of Chinese
                          who work ivory like silk
                          is not to be taken lightly . . .

11 April

I caught the name of the Chinese who comes every day:
                              SI-YA-U

16 April

Today we spoke with him
in the language of eyes.
He works as a weaver days
and studies nights.
Now it's a long time since the night
came on like a pack of black-shirted Fascists.
The cry of a man out of work
who threw himself into the Seine
rose from the dark water.
And ah you on whose fist-size head
                  mountainlike winds descend,
at this very minute you're probably busy
building towers of thick, leather-bound books
to get answers to the answers you asked of the stars.

Read
SI-YA-U
    READ . . .
And when your eyes find in the lines what it is they desire
                                when your eyes tire
rest your tired head
            like a black yellow Japanese chrysanthemum
                            on the books . . .
                            SLEEP
                                SI-YA-U
                                    SLEEP...

18 April

I began to forget
the names of the plump Renaissance masters.
I want to see
        the black bird-and-flower
                            watercolors
            that slant-eyed Chinese painters
                            drip
            from their long thin bamboo brushes.

NEWS FROM THE PARIS WIRELESS

        HALLO
            HALLO
                HALLO
        PARIS
            PARIS
                PARIS . . .
Voices race through the air
                like fiery greyhounds.
The wireless in the Eiffel Tower calls out:
        HALLO
            HALLO
                HALLO
        PARIS
            PARIS
                PARIS . . .

"WE TOO are Orientals, this voice is for us.
Our ears too are a receiver.
We too must listen to Eiffel."
News from China
                    News from China
                                        News from China:
The dragon that came down from the Kaf Mountains
                                        has spread his wings
across the golden skies of the Chinese homeland.
But
in this business it's not only the British lord's
gullet shaved
                    like the thick neck
                                        of a plucked hen
that will be cut
but also
          the long
                    thin
                              beard of Confucius!

FROM GIOCONDA'S DIARY

21 April

Today my Chinese
                    looked me straight
                                        in the eye
and asked:
"Those who crush our rice fields
          with the caterpillar treads of their tanks
and who swagger through our cities
          like emperors of hell,
are they of YOUR race,
          the race of him who CREATED you?"
I almost raised my hand
          and cried "No!"

27 April

     Tonight at the sound of an American trumpet
the horn of a 12-horsepower Ford
                    I woke up from a dream,
and what I saw in an instant
                 died in an instant.
What I saw was a still blue lake.
In this lake the slant-eyed light of my life
     had wrapped his fingers around the neck of a gilded fish.
I was going to him,
my boat a Chinese teacup.
I spread a sail
         of the embroidered silk
             of a bamboo
                 Japanese umbrella . . .

NEWS FROM THE PARIS WIRELESS

     HALLO
         HALLO
             HALLO
    PARIS
        PARIS
            PARIS
The radio station signs off.
Once more
          the blue-shirted Parisians fill
              Paris with red voices
                  and red colors . . .

FROM GIOCONDA'S DIARY

2 May

Today my Chinese failed to show up.

17

5 May

Still no sign of him . . .

8 May

My days
                like the waiting room
                                        of a station:
Eyes glued
                to the tracks . . .

10 May

Sculptors of Greece,
painters of Seljuk china,
weavers of rugs out of fire in Persia,
chanters of hymns to dromedaries in deserts,
dancer whose body undulates like the breeze,
craftsman who wrings 36 sides from a one-carat stone,
and YOU
                who carry five talents on your five fingers
                                master MICHELANGELO!
Cry out and announce to both friend and foe:
Because he made too much noise in Paris,
because he smashed in the window
                                of the Mandarin ambassador,
        Gioconda's lover
                        has been kicked out
                                        of France . . .
My lover from China has gone back to China . . .
And now I'd like to know
who's Romeo and Juliet!
But if he isn't Juliet in pants
                and I'm not Romeo in skirts—
If I could only cry . . . Ah,
                        if I could cry . . .

12 May

Today
    when I caught a glimpse of myself
        in the mirror of this mother's daughter
touching up the paint
            on her bloody mouth
    in front of me,
    the tin crown of my fame shattered on my head.
While the desire to cry writhes inside me
                I smile demurely;
like a stuffed pig's head
           my ugly face grins on . . .
    Leonardo da Vinci,
        may your bones
           become the brush of a Cubist painter
for grabbing me by the throat—your hands dripping with
                      paint—
and sticking in my mouth like a gold-plated tooth
this cursed smile. . . .

End of Part One

Part Two
The Flight

FROM THE AUTHOR'S NOTEBOOK

Ah, friends, Gioconda is in a bad way . . .
Take it from me
      if she didn't have hopes
           of getting word from afar
she'd steal a guard's pistol
        and aiming to give the color of death
to her lips' cursed smile
        she'd empty it into her canvas breast . . .

FROM GIOCONDA'S DIARY

O that Leonardo da Vinci's brush
had conceived me
                    under the gilded sun of China!
That the painted mountain behind me
had been a sugar-loaf Chinese mountain,
that the pink-white color of my long face
                              could fade,
that my eyes could be almond-shaped!
And if only my smile
                    could show what I feel in my heart!
Then in the arms of him who is far away
            I could have wandered through China . . .

FROM THE AUTHOR'S NOTEBOOK

We had a heart-to-heart talk with Gioconda today.
The hours flew by
                    one after another
like the pages of a spellbinding book.
And we arrived at such a decision that
this decision
            is going to cut like a knife
                              Gioconda's life in two.
Tomorrow night you'll see us carry it out . . .

FROM THE AUTHOR'S NOTEBOOK

The clock of Notre Dame de Paris
                              strikes mid-night.
Mid-night
            mid-night.
Who knows at this very minute
            which drunk is killing his wife?
Who knows at this very minute
            which ghost
                        is roaming around in the halls
                                        of a castle?

Who knows at this very minute
            which thief
                        is surmounting
                              the most unsurmountable wall?
Mid-night . . . Mid-night . . .
Who knows at this very minute . . .
I know very well that in every novel
                        this is the darkest hour.
Mid-night
            strikes fear into the heart of every reader . . .
But what could I do?
When my monoplane landed
                  on the roof of the Louvre,
the clock of Notre Dame de Paris
                  struck mid-night.
And, strange to tell, feeling no fear,
I patted the aluminum rump of my plane
                              and stepped down on the roof . . .
Uncoiling the 50-fathom-long rope I'd wound around my
                                          waist,
I lowered it outside Gioconda's window
like a vertical bridge between heaven and hell.
I blew my shrill whistle three times.
And immediately I got a response
to those three shrill whistles.
Gioconda threw open her window.
This poor farmer's daughter
                        done up as the Virgin Mary
chucked her gilded frame
and grabbing hold of the rope pulled herself up . . .

SI-YA-U my friend
                  to tell the truth you were lucky
to fall to a lion-hearted woman like this . . .

FROM GIOCONDA'S DIARY

This thing that they call an airplane
                        is a winged iron horse.

Below us is Paris
          with its Eiffel Tower—
                    a sharp-nosed, pock-marked, moon-like face.
We're climbing
               we're climbing.
Like an arrow of fire
               we're piercing
                         the darkness.
The heavens rise overhead
                    as if coming closer;
the sky is like a meadowful of flowers.
               We're climbing
                         we're climbing.

.   .   .   .

     .   .   .   .

.   .   .   .

I must have dozed off
               I opened my eyes.
Dawn's moment of glory.
The skies a calm ocean,
our plane a ship.
I call this smooth sailing, smooth as butter.
Behind us a wake of smoke floats.
Our eyes are surveying blue vacancies
               full of glittering discs . . .
Below us the earth is like
          a Jaffa orange
                    turning gold in the sun . . .
By what magic is it that I
          have climbed up from the ground
                    the height of hundreds of minarets,
and yet to look down at the earth
          my mouth still waters . . .

FROM THE AUTHOR'S NOTEBOOK

Now our plane swims
           within the hot winds
                     that swarm over Africa.
Seen from above
           Africa looks like a huge violin.
I swear
they're playing Tchaikovsky on a cello
                     on the angry dark island
                               of Africa.
And waving his long hairy arms
           a gorilla is sobbing . . .

FROM THE AUTHOR'S NOTEBOOK

We're passing over Indian waters.
We're drinking the air
           like a heavy, faint-smelling syrup.
And keeping our eyes on the yellow beacon of Singapore—
leaving Australia on the right,
           Madagascar on the left—
and placing our faith in the fuel in the tank,
           we headed for the China Sea . . .

       *From the journals of a deckhand named John aboard
a British vessel in the China Sea*

That night
       a typhoon blew up out of the blue.
Man,
       what a hurricane!
Mounted on the back of a yellow devil, the Mother of God
           whirls around and around, stirring up the air.
And as luck would have it
           I had the watch on the foretop.
The huge ship under me
           looks about this big!

The wind is roaring
        blast after
                blast
                        blast after
                                blast . . .
The mast quivers like a strung bow.(*)
Oops, now we're going all the way up
                my head splits the clouds.
Oops, now we're sinking all the way down
                my fingers comb the ocean floor.
We're leaning to the left, we're leaning to the right.
That is, we're leaning larboard and starboard.
My God, we just sank!
                Oh no! This time we're sure to go under.
The waves
leap over my head
                like Bengal tigers.
Fear
        leads me on
                like a coffee-colored Javanese whore.
This is no joke, this is the China Sea . . . (**)

Okay, let's keep it short.
PLOP . . .
What's that?
A rectangular piece of canvas dropped from the air
                                into the crow's nest.
This canvas
        was some kind of woman!
It occurred to me that this madame who came from the skies
                wouldn't know what to make
                        of our seamen's talk and ways.
I got right down and kissed her hand

(*) What business do you have being way up there?
        Christ, man, what do you think you are, a stork?
                N. H.
(**) The deckhand has every right to be afraid.
        The rage of the China Sea is not to be taken lightly.
                N. H.

and using the mouth of a poet I cried:
"O you canvas-woman who came to me from the skies!
Tell me, which goddess should I compare you to?
Why did you descend here? What is your large purpose?"
She replied:
"I fell

        from a 550-horsepower plane.
My name is Gioconda,
        I'm from Florence.
I must arrive in the port of Shanghai
        as soon as possible."

FROM GIOCONDA'S DIARY

The wind died down
    the sea calmed down.
The ship makes strides toward Shanghai.
The sailors dream,
        rocking in their sailcloth hammocks.
A song of Indian waters flickers
        on their thick, fleshy lips:
"The fire of the Cochin-China sun
warms the blood
    like Malacca wine.
They draw sailors to gilded stars,
        those Cochin-China nights,
        those Cochin-China nights.

Slant-eyed yellow Bornese cabin boys
knifed in Singapore bars
painted the iron-belted barrels blood-red.
Those Cochin-China nights, those Cochin-China nights.

A ship plunges on to Canton
55,000 tons
those Cochin-China nights . . .

As the moon swims in the heavens
      like the corpse of a blue-eyed sailor
        thrown overboard,
Bombay watches, leaning on its elbow . . .
              Bombay moon,
                Arabian Sea.

The fire of the Cochin-China sun
warms the blood
      like Malacca wine.
They draw sailors to gilded stars,
        those Cochin-China nights,
          those Cochin-China nights . . ."

End of Part Two

Part Three
Gioconda's End

THE CITY OF SHANGHAI

Shanghai is a big port,
an excellent port.
Its ships are taller than
horned Mandarin mansions.
My, my!
What a strange place, this Shanghai . . .

In the blue river float
boats with straw sails.
In those boats with straw sails
naked coolies sort rice,
        raving of rice . . .
My, my!
What a strange place, this Shanghai . . .

Shanghai is a big port.
The ships of the whites are huge,
the boats of the yellows are tiny.

Shanghai is pregnant with a red-headed child.
My, my!

FROM THE AUTHOR'S NOTEBOOK

Last night
when the ship entered the harbor
Gioconda's foot kissed the land.
Shanghai the soup, she the ladle,
she searched high and low for her SI-YA-U.

FROM THE AUTHOR'S NOTEBOOK

"Chinese work! Japanese work!
Only two people make this—
one man, one woman.

Chinese work! Japanese work!
Just look at the art
in this latest work of LI-LI-FU."

Screaming at the top of his voice
the Chinese magician
                    LI.
His shriveled yellow spider of a hand
is tossing long thin knives into the air:
That's one
            one more
                    one more
                            one more
                                    that's five
                                            one more.
Tracing lightninglike circles in the air
six knives fly up in a steady stream.
Gioconda looks on,
                she keeps looking,
                        she'd still be looking but
like a large-colored Chinese lantern
                the crowd swayed and became confused:

"Stand back! Make way!
Chiang Kai-shek's executioner
                is hunting down a new head.
Stand back! Make way!"

One in front and one close behind
two Chinese sprang around the corner.
The one in front runs toward Gioconda.
This one racing toward her, it was him, it was him, yes, him!
Her SI-YA-U
              her dove.
                    SI-YA-U . . .
A dull hollow stadium sound surrounded them.
And in the cruel English language
                    painted red with the blood
                              of yellow Asia
                                   the crowd cried out:
"He's catching up
he's catching up
          he caught—
                    catch him!"

Just three steps away from Gioconda's arms
Chiang Kai-shek's executioner caught up.
The sword
          flashed . . .
Thud of cut flesh and bone.
Like a yellow sun drenched in blood
SI-YA-U's head
                    fell at her feet . . .
And thus on a death-day
Gioconda of Florence lost in Shanghai
her smile more famous than Florence.

FROM THE AUTHOR'S NOTEBOOK

A Chinese bamboo frame.
In the frame is a painting.
Under the painting, a name:

La Gioconda . . .
In the frame is a painting:
      the eyes of the painting in the frame are burning,
               burning.
In the frame is a painting:
      the painting in the frame is coming alive,
              coming alive.
And suddenly
    as if jumping out of a window
        the painting sprang out of the frame;
          her feet hit the ground.
And just as I was shouting her name
she stood up straight before me:
     the giant woman of a colossal struggle.

She walked on ahead
    I trailed behind.
From the blazing red Tibetan sun
to the China Sea
      we went and came,
      we came and went.
I saw
    Gioconda
        sneaking out under the cover of darkness
through the gates of a city in enemy hands;
I saw her
in a skirmish of drawn bayonets
        wringing the neck of a British officer.
I saw her
at the head of a blue stream swimming with stars
washing the lice from her dirty shirt . . .

Huffing and puffing, a wood-burning engine
is dragging behind it
forty red cars seating forty people each.
The cars passed by one after another.
In the last car I saw her
keeping watch:
      a frayed lambskin hat on her head,

boots on her feet,
a leather jacket on her back . . .

FROM THE AUTHOR'S NOTEBOOK

Ah, my patient readers!
Now with you we
find ourselves in the French military court in Shanghai.
The judges:
Four generals, fourteen colonels,
and an armed black Congolese regiment.
The accused:
Gioconda.
The attorney for the defense:
An excessively crazed—
that is, excessively artistic—
                      French painter.
The scene is set.
                 We're starting:

The attorney for the defense presents his case:

"Gentlemen,
this masterpiece
      that stands in your presence as the accused
is the most accomplished daughter of a great artist.
Gentlemen,
      this masterpiece . . .
Gentlemen . . .
My mind is on fire . . .
Gentlemen . . .
      Renaissance . . .
Gentlemen . . .
      this masterpiece,
            twice this masterpiece . . .
Gentlemen, uniformed gentlemen . . ."
"C-U-U-U-T!
            Enough.
Stop sputtering like a jammed machine gun.

Recording clerk,
           read the verdict."

The recording clerk reads the verdict:

"The law of France
           has been violated in China
by the above-named Gioconda, daughter of Leonardo.
Accordingly,
           we judged
                      appropriate the burning
                                 of the accused.
And tomorrow night as the moon comes up
a Senegalese regiment
                      will execute this decision
                                 of our military court . . ."

THE BURNING

Shanghai is a big port.
The ships of the whites are huge.
The boats of the yellows are tiny.
A thick whistle.
                      A thin Chinese scream.
A ship steaming into the harbor
                      capsized a straw-sailed boat . . .
Moonlight.
Night.
Handcuffed,
           Gioconda waits.
Blow, wind, blow . . .
A voice:
"All right, the lighter.
Burn Gioconda, burn . . ."
A silhouette advances
a flash . . .
They lit the lighter
and set fire to Gioconda.
Gioconda was painted red by the flames.

She laughed with a smile that came from her heart.
Gioconda burned laughing . . .

Art, Shmart, Masterpiece, Shmasterpiece, And So On, And So
Forth,
Immortality, Eternity

H-E-E-E-E-E-E-E-E-E-E-Y . . .

**"HERE ENDS OUR TALE'S CONTENDING
THE REST IS LIES UNENDING . . ."**
THE END

1929

2

Poems from Prison

1

I carved your name on my watchband
with my fingernail.
Where I am, you know,
there's neither a pearl-handled jackknife
(they don't give us anything sharp)
           nor a sycamore with its head in the clouds.
Maybe there's a tree in the yard,
but to see the sky overhead
                      is forbidden for me . . .
How many people besides me are in this place?
I don't know.
I'm alone far from them,
they're all together far from me.
To talk to anyone other than myself
                      is forbidden.
So I talk to myself.
But I find my conversation so boring,
           my dear wife, that I sing songs.
And what do you know,
that awful, always off-key voice of mine
           touches me so
                that my heart breaks.
And just like the barefoot orphan
     lost in the snow
in those old sad stories, my heart
—with moist blue eyes
and a little red runny nose—
           wants to snuggle up in your arms.
It doesn't make me blush
           that my heart right now
                is this weak,
                    this selfish,
                      this *human* simply.
There's probably a physiological, psychological, etc.

explanation for my state.
Or perhaps it's
        this barred window,
          this earthen jug,
            these four walls,
        which for months have kept me from hearing
        another human voice.

It's five o'clock, my dear.
Outside, with its dryness,
         its eerie whispering,
           its mud roof,
and with its lame, skinny horse
        that stands motionless in the midst of infinity
—I mean it's enough to drive the man inside crazy with grief—
outside, with all its machinery and all its art,
a plains night comes down red on treeless space.
Again today it will be night in no time.
A light will circle the lame, skinny horse.
And the treeless space, in this hopeless landscape
that's stretched out before me like the body of a hard man,
will suddenly be filled with stars.
It means we've reached the expected end once more,
which is to say everything is in its place, everything is ready
again today for an elaborate nostalgia.
Me,
the man inside,
once more I'll exhibit my customary talent,
and in the reedy voice of my childhood
singing an old-fashioned lament,
once more, by God, it will crush my unhappy heart
to hear you inside my head,
so far
away, as if I were watching you
            in a smoky, broken mirror . . .

2

Outside, spring has come, my dear, spring.
Outside on the plains, suddenly
the smell of fresh earth, birds singing, etc.
Spring, it's spring outside, my dear wife,
outside on the plains it's sparkling . . .
And inside the bed is coming alive with its bugs,
                          the water jug no longer freezes,
and in the morning there's sun on the concrete . . .
The sun—
every day until noon these days
it comes and goes
from me, flashing off
                  and on . . .
And as the day turns to afternoon, shadows fall on the walls,
the glass of the barred window starts to catch fire,
                          and outside it's night,
                          a cloudless spring night . . .
And inside it's truly the darkest hour of the spring.
In short,
it's especially in spring that the demon called freedom
—with its glittering sequin-skin and eyes of fire—
                          possesses the man inside . . .
This is proven by experience, my dear wife,
                  proven by experience . . .

3

Sunday today.
Today they took me out in the sun for the first time.
And I stood very still, struck for the first time in my life
                          by how far away the sky is,
                          how blue
                          and how wide.
Then I respectfully sat down on the earth.
I put my back against the wall.
For a moment no trap to fall into,
for a moment no struggle, no freedom, no wife.
Just earth, sun, and me . . .
I am happy.   1938

THE WORLD, MY FRIENDS, MY ENEMIES, YOU, AND THE EARTH

I'm wonderfully happy I came into the world,
I love its earth, its light, its struggle, and its bread.
Even though I know its dimensions from pole to pole to the
centimeter,
and while I'm not unaware that it's a mere toy next to the sun,
the world for me is unbelievably big.
I would have liked to go around the world
and see the fish, the fruits, and the stars that I haven't
seen.
However,
I made my European trip only in books and pictures.
In all my life I never got one letter
with its blue stamp canceled in Asia.
Me and our corner grocer,
we're both mightily unknown in America.
Nevertheless,
from China to Spain, from the Cape of Good Hope to Alaska,
in every nautical mile, in every kilometer, I have friends
and enemies.
Such friends that we haven't met even once—
we can die for the same bread, the same freedom, the same
dream.
And such enemies that they're thirsty for my blood,
I am thirsty for their blood.
My strength
is that I'm not alone in this big world.
The world and its people are no secret in my heart,
no mystery in my science.
Calmly and openly
I took my place
in the great struggle.
And without it,
you and the earth
are not enough for me.
And yet you are astonishingly beautiful,
the earth is warm and beautiful.   1939

They who are numberless
                    like ants in the earth,
                              fish in the sea,
                                        birds in the air,
who are cowardly,
                    brave,
                              ignorant,
                                        wise,
                                        and childlike,
and who destroy
                    and create, they—
our epic tells only of their adventures.

They who fall for the traitor's lie
                              and drop their banner on the ground
and leaving the field to the enemy
                              run inside their houses
and who pull their knives on the renegade
and who laugh like a green tree
and cry without ceremony
and who swear like hell,
our epic tells only of their adventures.

The destiny
                    of iron,
                              coal,
                                        and sugar,
of red copper
and textiles
and love and cruelty and life
and all the branches of industry
and the sky
                    and the desert
                              and the blue ocean,
of sad riverbeds,
and of plowed earth and cities
          will be changed one morning,

one morning when, at the edge of darkness,
                pushing against the earth with their heavy hands,
                                        they stand up.

They are the ones
        who inspire the brightest shapes in the most knowing
                                                mirrors.
In this century they were victorious, they were defeated.
Many things have been said about them,
and about them
                it was said
        they have nothing to lose but their chains.

Nazim, what happiness
that, open and confident,
you could say "Hello"
from the bottom of your heart.

The year is 1940.
The month, July.
The day is the first Thursday of the month.
The hour: 9.

Date your letters in detail like this.
We're living in such a world
        that the month, the day, and the hour
          contain more writing than the thickest book.

Hello, everybody.

To say a big
        fat "Hello"
and then, without finishing my sentence,
        to look at you with a smile
—sly and gleeful—
        and wink . . .

We're such perfect friends
        that we understand each other
          without words or writing . . .

Hello, everybody,
hello to all of you . . .

"The plum trees
        are in bloom
—the wild apricot flowers first,
                the plum last—

My love,
let's sit
face to face
on the grass.
The air is delicious and light
—but not really warm yet—
the almond shells are green
            and fuzzy, still
                    very soft . . .
We're happy
        because we're alive.
We'd probably have been killed long ago
if you were in London,
if I were in Tobruk or on an English freighter . . .

Put your hands on your knees, my love
—your wrists thick and white—
and open your left hand:
the daylight is inside your palm
            like an apricot . . .
Of the people killed in yesterday's air raid,
        about one hundred were under five,
twenty-four still babies . . .

I love the color of pomegranate seeds, my love
—a pomegranate seed, seed of light—
I like melons fragrant,
my plums tart . . ."

. . . . . . a rainy day
far from fruits and you

—not a single tree has bloomed yet,
and there's even a chance of snow—
in Bursa Prison,
carried away by a strange feeling
and about to explode,
I write this out of pigheadedness—
out of sheer spite—for myself and for the people I love.

2.7.1941

They've taken us prisoner,
they've thrown us in jail:
              me inside the walls,
                      you outside.
But this is nothing.
The worst thing
is for a person—knowingly or not—
to carry prison inside himself . . .
Most people have been forced into this position,
honest, hard-working, good people,
who deserve to be loved as much as I love you.

The trees on the plain are making one last effort to shine:
                          spangled gold
                             copper
                                bronze and wood . . .
The feet of the oxen sink softly into the damp earth.
And the mountains are dipped in smoke:
                        lead-gray, soaking wet . . .
That's it,
fall must be finally over today.
Wild geese just shot by,
                     they're probably headed for Iznik Lake.
In the air, a coolness,
     in the air, something like the smell of soot:
     the smell of snow is in the air.

To be outside now,
          to ride a horse at full gallop toward the mountains . . .
You'll say, "You don't know how to ride a horse,"
but don't joke
          and don't be jealous:
I've acquired a new habit in prison,
I love nature—if not as much,
          nearly as much—as I love you.
          And both of you are far away.

ABOUT MOUNT ULUDAĞ

For seven years now Uludağ and I have been staring each
                              other in the eye.
It hasn't moved an inch,
             and neither have I,
yet we know each other well.
Like all living things, it knows how to laugh and how to
                                  get mad.

Sometimes,
      in winter, especially at night,
             when the wind blows from the south,
with its snowy forests, plateaus, and frozen lakes
            it turns over in its sleep,
and the Old Man who lives way up there at the very top—
         his long beard flying,
               skirts billowing—
      rides howling on the wind down into the valley . . .

Then sometimes,
      especially in May, at sunup,
      it rises like a brand-new world—
         huge, blue, vast,
         free and happy.

Then there are days
      when it looks like its picture on the pop bottles.
And then I understand that in its hotel I can't see
         lady skiers sipping cognac
         are flirting with the gentlemen skiers.

And the day comes
when one of its beetle-browed mountain folk, having
butchered his neighbor at the altar of sacred property,
         comes to us as a guest in his yellow homespun trousers
            to do fifteen years in cellblock 71.

                                  1947

SINCE I WAS THROWN INSIDE

Since I was thrown inside
    the earth has gone around the sun ten times.
If you ask it:
            "Not worth mentioning—
                a microscopic span."
If you ask me:
            "Ten years of my life."

I had a pencil
            the year I was thrown inside.
It was used up after a week of writing.
If you ask it:
            "A whole lifetime."
If you ask me:
            "What's a week."

Since I've been inside,
    Osman, who was in for murder,
                did his seven-and-a-half and left,
                knocked around on the outside for a while,
                then landed back inside for smuggling,
                served six months and was out again;
                yesterday we got a letter—he's married,
                with a kid coming in the spring.

They're ten-years-old now,
    the children who were conceived
            the year I was thrown inside.
And that year's foals—shaky on their long, spindly legs—
    have been wide-rumped, contented mares for some time
                                now.
But the olive seedlings are still saplings,
                still children.

New squares have opened in my faraway city
                since I was thrown inside.
And my family now lives

on a street I don't know,
in a house I haven't seen.

Bread was like cotton—soft and white—
the year I was thrown inside.
Then it was rationed,
and here inside people killed each other
over a black loaf the size of a fist.
Now it's free again,
but it's dark and has no taste.

The year I was thrown inside
the SECOND hadn't started yet.
The ovens at Dachau hadn't been lit,
the atom bomb hadn't been dropped on Hiroshima.

Time flowed like blood from the slit throat of a child.
Then that chapter was officially closed—
now the American dollar is talking of a THIRD.

But in spite of everything the day has gotten lighter
since I was thrown inside.
And "at the edge of darkness,
pushing against the earth with their heavy hands,
THEY've risen up" halfway.

Since I was thrown inside
the earth has gone around the sun ten times.
And I repeat once more with the same passion
what I wrote about Them
the year I was thrown inside:
"They who are numberless like ants in the earth,
fish in the sea,
birds in the air,
who are cowardly, brave,
ignorant, wise,
and childlike,
and who destroy
and create, they—

our songs tell only of their adventures."
And anything else,
such as my ten years here,
is just so much talk.

1947

ANGINA PECTORIS

If half my heart is here, doctor,
        the other half is in China
with the army flowing
        toward the Yellow River.
And every morning, doctor,
every morning at sunrise my heart
        is shot in Greece.
And every night, doctor,
when the prisoners are asleep and the infirmary is deserted,
my heart stops at a run-down old house
                                in Istanbul.
And then after ten years
all I have to offer my poor people
is this apple in my hand, doctor,
one red apple:
                my heart.
And that, doctor, that is the reason
for this angina pectoris—
not nicotine, prison, or arteriosclerosis.
I look at the night through the bars,
and despite the weight on my chest
my heart still beats with the most distant stars.

                                        1948

You're like a scorpion, my brother,
you live in cowardly darkness
                              like a scorpion.
You're like a sparrow, my brother,
always in a sparrow's flutter.
You're like a clam, my brother,
closed like a clam, content.
And you're frightening, my brother, like the mouth of an
                              extinct volcano.
Not one,
     not five,
you are millions, unfortunately.
You're like a sheep, my brother.
                    When the cloaked drover raises his stick,
                         you quickly join the herd
and run, almost proudly, to the slaughterhouse.
I mean, you're the strangest creature on earth—
stranger, even, than that fish
                    that couldn't see the ocean for the water.
And the oppression in this world
                         is thanks to you.
And if we're hungry, if we're tired, if we're covered with
                              blood,
and if we're still being crushed like grapes for our wine,
                              the fault is yours
—I can hardly bring myself to say it—
but most of the fault, my dear brother, is yours.

                                        1949

SOME ADVICE TO THOSE WHO WILL SERVE TIME IN PRISON

If instead of being hanged by the neck
        you're thrown inside
        for not giving up hope
in the world, in your country, in people,
      if you do ten or fifteen years
      apart from the time you have left,
you won't say
          "Better I had swung from the end of a rope
                  like a flag"—
you'll put your foot down and live.
It might not be a pleasure exactly,
but it's your solemn duty
        to live one more day
            to spite the enemy.
Part of you may live alone inside,
        like a stone at the bottom of a well.
But the other part
        must be so caught up
        in the flurry of the world
        that you shiver there inside
      when outside, at forty days' distance, a leaf moves.
To wait for letters inside,
or to sing sad songs,
or to lie awake all night staring at the ceiling
        is sweet, but dangerous.
Look at your face from shave to shave,
forget your age,
watch out for lice,
        and for spring nights;
    and always remember
        to eat every last piece of bread—
also, don't forget to laugh heartily.
And, who knows,
the woman you love may no longer love you.
Don't say it's no big thing—

52

it's like the snapping of a green branch
                              to the man inside.
To think of roses and gardens inside is bad,
to think of seas and mountains is good.
Read and write without stopping to rest,
and I also advise weaving,
and also making mirrors.
I mean it's not that you can't pass
        ten or fifteen years inside,
                and more even—
            you can,
            as long as the jewel
            in the left side of your chest doesn't lose its luster!

                                    May 1949

I

Living is no laughing matter:
        you must live with great seriousness
                like a squirrel, for example—
I mean without looking for something beyond and
                      above living,
        I mean living must be your whole occupation.
Living is no laughing matter:
        you must take it seriously,
        so much so and to such a degree that,
    for example, your hands tied behind your back, your
                    back to the wall,
    or else in a laboratory
        in your white coat and thick glasses,
        you'll be able to die for people—
    even for people whose faces you've never seen,
    even though you know living
        is the most real, the most beautiful thing.
I mean you must take living so seriously
    that even at seventy, for example, you will plant olives—
    and not so they'll be left for your children either,
    but because even though you fear death you don't
                    believe it,
    because living, I mean, weighs heavier.

II

Let's say we're seriously ill, need surgery—
which is to say there's a chance we won't get up
                from the white table.
Even though it's impossible not to feel sad about going a
                  little too soon,
we'll still laugh at the jokes being told,
we'll look out the window to see if it's raining,
or we'll still wait anxiously
              for the latest newscast . . .
Let's say we're at the front,

for something worth fighting for, say.
There, in the first offensive, on that very day,
                we might fall on our face, dead.
We'll know this with a curious anger,
        but we'll still worry ourselves to death
        about the outcome of the war, which might go on for
                                        years.

Let's say we're in prison
and close to fifty,
and we have eighteen more years, say, before the iron doors
                                        will open.
We'll still live with the outside,
with its people and animals, struggle and wind—
                I mean with the outside beyond the walls.
I mean, however and wherever we are,
        we must live as if one never dies.

III
This earth will grow cold,
a star among stars
                and one of the smallest—
a gilded mote on the blue velvet, I mean,
        I mean *this,* our great earth.
This earth will grow cold one day,
not like a heap of ice
or a dead cloud even,
but like an empty walnut it will roll along
                in pitch-black space . . .
You must grieve for this right now,
you have to feel this sorrow now,
for the world must be loved this much
                if you're going to say "I lived" . . .

1948

3

Late Poems

You woke up.
Where are you?
At home.
You're still
        not used to waking up
        in your own house.
This is the kind of daze
        thirteen years of prison leaves you in.
Who's sleeping next to you?
It's not loneliness—it's your wife.
She's sleeping peacefully, like an angel.
Pregnancy becomes the lady.
What time is it?
Eight.
You're safe till night.
Because it's the custom:
        the police don't raid houses in broad daylight.

1950

You no sooner got out of prison
than you made your wife
        pregnant;
she's on your arm,
      and you're out for an evening walk around the
                      neighborhood.
The lady's belly comes up to her nose.
She carries her sacred charge coyly.
You're respectful and proud.
The air is cool
—cool like baby hands.
You'd like to take it in your palms
        and warm it up.
The neighborhood cats are at the butcher's door,
and upstairs his curly wife
has settled her breasts on the window ledge
             and is watching the evening.
Half-light, spotless sky:
smack in the middle sits the evening star,
        sparkling like a glass of water.
Indian summer lasted long this year—
the mulberry trees are yellow,
          but the figs are still green.
Refik the typesetter and the milkman Yorgi's middle daughter
      have gone out for an evening stroll,
        their fingers locked.
The grocer Karabet's lights are on.
This Armenian citizen has not forgiven
      the slaughter of his father in the Kurdish mountains.
But he loves you,
because you also won't forgive
      those who blackened the name of the Turkish
                people.
The tuberculars of the neighborhood and the bedridden
     look out from behind the glass.

The washwoman Huriye's unemployed son,
                    weighed down by his sadness,
                         goes off to the coffeehouse.
Rahmi Bey's radio is giving the news:
in a country in the Far East,
moon-faced yellow people
          are fighting a white dragon.
Of your people,
          four thousand five hundred Mehmets
               have been sent there to murder their brothers.
You blush
          with rage and shame
and not in general either—
     this impotent grief
     is all yours.
It's as if they'd knocked your wife down from behind
                         and killed her child,
or as if you were back in jail
and they were making the peasant guards
                         beat the peasants again.

All of a sudden it's night.
The evening walk is over.
A police jeep turned into your street,
your wife whispered:
               "To our house?"

                                   1950

You're a field,
    I am the tractor.
You're paper,
    I am the typewriter.
My wife, mother of my son,
you're a song—
    I am the guitar.
I am the warm, humid night the south wind brings—
    you're the woman walking by the water
        looking across at the lights.
I'm water—
    you are the drinker.
I'm the passerby on the road,
    you are the one who opens her window
        to beckon to me.
You're China,
    I am Mao Tse-tung's army.
You're a young Filipino girl 14-years-old,
    I rescue you
        from the hands of an American sailor.
You're a mountain village
    in Anatolia,
you're my city,
    most beautiful and most unhappy.
You're a cry for help, I mean you're my country;
    the steps running toward you—that's me.

1951

BALCONY

In Kurort-Varna, I'm looking out from the balcony of the
                                        Balkan-Tourist:
street, trees,
        beyond them sand,
beyond that must be sea and sky
no
        neither sea nor sky,
beyond the sand is simply light,
        no end of light . . .
And there's this smell of roses in the air
that burns the nostrils.
I don't see any roses,
but I can tell from the odor
that they're all enormous,
        all very red . . .
The Polish tourists flock down to the beach,
blond, pink, half-naked . . .
A swallow spins overhead:
black wings, white breast.
He's not in the least like a bee,
but he's like a bee just the same.
Now you see him, now you don't
as he plunges and soars, giddy
        with his own song . . .
Cacik in a blue bowl.
They brought cheese *pide*
—it's as if I'm in Istanbul—
they brought cheese *pide*
with sesame seeds, soft, steaming . . .
This summer day in Varna,
all big words aside,
even for a very sick, very exiled poet
this happiness to be alive.

My dear,
I'm writing this lying down,
I'm so tired.
I saw my face in the mirror—I look green.
The weather is cold, summer will never come.
We need thirty liras of wood each week,
                    it's not easy to manage.
A while ago, when I was working at
the table, I had to put a blanket on my back.
The glass, the frames are broken,
the doors won't close,
it's impossible to live here any more,
                    we'll have to move,
the house is going to come crumbling down on us.
But rents are awfully high . . .
Why am I telling you all this?
You'll worry,
but to whom else should I pour out my troubles?
Forgive me.

If it would just get warm, *real* warm,
                    especially nights.
I'm sick and tired of being cold.
In my dreams I go to Africa.
One time I was in Algiers.
It was hot.
A bullet pierced my forehead.
All my blood gushed out,
                    but I didn't die . . .
Something has come over me,
I suddenly feel very old
—yet you know
          I'm not even forty—
I feel as if I'm very old.
I say it, too,
and when I say it, they get mad—

I get lectured by everybody.
Anyway, let's drop this subject . . .

They made a movie of Chekhov's "La Cigale."
It was shown in Paris. Everyone liked it.
Is it all that poor, silly woman's fault?
I both like the doctor
                    and can't forgive the bastard.
In the end, who's more unhappy?
                    Who, and because of whom?

The radio played some Paraguayan folk songs.
They were written on rough leaves
with love, the sun, and human sweat,
at once bitter and hopeful.
I liked the Paraguayan songs.

I got a letter from Adviye,
she says she misses me very much,
says she can't forget me.
I was stunned.
For years,
since you fled the country,
she neither knocked on my door
                    nor so much as sent word.
We even met on the street
one holiday morning,
she turned her head and walked right by.
We were the closest friends.
But friendship is like a tree:
once it dries up,
                    it can't bloom again.
I didn't answer—
what good would it do?
Even if she comes to my house now,
I have nothing to say to her.
I have nothing against her either.
Let her live happily ever after.
I hear she found a rich husband,
the man's a sickly thing,

and a maniac too,
yet Adviye was such a lively woman . . .

I just checked our son—
he's sound asleep, rosy and blond.
His blanket was off. I covered him up.
The radio also gave some bad news tonight,
Irène Joliot-Curie died.
She was still young.
Years ago
I read a book
about her mother.
In one place it talked about two daughters,
I can still see the lines—
Like two blond Greek statues, it said.
And now one of those children is dead.
How shall I say this,
a great scientist, a great person,
but she's also that blond little girl
who's now dead of leukemia.
This death shook me,
I cried tonight
                for Irène Joliot-Curie.
If they'd said,
            Irène, how strange,
                Irène, if they'd said,
                    when you're dead,
a woman in Istanbul,
someone you don't know at all,
will cry for you—
                if they'd said—
                    she'd have laughed.
I thought of her husband,
if I wrote a letter
and sent him my condolences,
                    I thought.
But I don't know his address.
If I'd said, Paris. Frédéric Joliot,
                    would it have gone?

66

A French writer also died,
I read it in the paper.
I'm sure you've never heard of him.
Anyway he was very old,
and an egotist on top of it—
                    a cowering,
                    nasty fellow.
He spent his whole life mocking everything,
he didn't love anyone or anything
but dogs and cats
and then only his own.
He gave an interview a couple days before he died,
he thinks he's mocking death
but it's clear that he's awfully scared.
There's a picture of him, too—
make our grandmother a man
and put a skullcap on his head,
                    and there you have him.
A skinny old man
                    totally alone.
I felt sorry for him too.
Maybe because he looked like our grandmother,
                    or maybe it was his loneliness.
I pitied him,
but it's not the same.
One feels sorry for Irène Curie,
one thinks of her children, her husband,
but beyond that you feel sorry for the world
                    because a great person is dead.

I have some good news for you,
your lazy son is learning to read.
The rascal has made great progress:
hold, run, book, pen, bag . . .
Not bad, eh?
He likens each letter to something;
A is a house,
        B is a fat man,
                    T is a hammer.

I'm so scared he's going to turn out lazy.
I'm always trying to find work for him.
If he was a girl, it would be easy.
A woman can do any kind of work at any age.
But a five-year-old boy—
                    what work can he do?

Ah, if the weather would just warm up . . .
It *will* warm up!
My letter has gotten longer and longer,
take good care of yourself,
write to me right away,
don't forget me.
Write to me right away.
Don't fool yourself, saying,
Münevver's smart,
whatever happens she'll manage, etc.
I'm lost without you.
Don't forget me.
Take good care of yourself.
I kiss your eyes, my dear.
Good night.
Take good care of yourself.
Write to me right away.
Don't worry yourself about my troubles,
                    forget them.
                    Don't forget me . . .

                                        1956

Fall morning in the vineyard:
    in row after row the repetition of knotty vines,
        of clusters on the vines,
        of grapes in the clusters,
        of light on the grapes.

At night, in the big white house,
        the repetition of windows,
        each lit up separately.

The repetition of all the rain that rains
        on earth, tree, sea,
        my hands, my face, my eyes,
        and of the drops crushed on the glass.

The repetition of my days
        that are alike,
        my days that are not alike.

The repetition of the weave in the weaving,
        the repetition in the starry sky,
        and the repetition of "I love" in all languages.
        The repetition of the tree in the leaves
        and of the pain of living, which ends in an instant
            on every deathbed.

The repetition in the snow—
        in the light snow,
        in the heavy wet snow,
        in the dry snow,
the repetition in the snow that whirls
in the blizzard and drives me off the road.

The children are running in the courtyard,
in the courtyard the children are running.

An old woman is passing by on the street,
on the street, an old woman is passing by,
passing by on the street is an old woman.

At night, in the big white house,
        the repetition of windows,
        each lit up separately.

In the clusters, of grapes,
on the grapes, of light.

To walk toward the good, the just, the true,
to fight for the good, the just, the true,
to seize the good, the just, the true.
Your silent tears and smile, my rose,
your sobs and bursts of laughter, my rose,
the repetition of your shining white teeth when you laugh.

Fall morning in the vineyard:
        in row after row the repetition of knotty vines,
           of clusters on the vines,
           of grapes in the clusters,
           of light on the grapes,
           of my heart in the light.

My rose, this is the miracle of repetition—
to repeat without repeating.

The last bus at midnight
the conductor hands me a ticket.
Neither bad news nor a big dinner
          is waiting for me at home.
For me, absence waits.
I approach it without fear
          and without sadness.
The last dark is dawning for me.
At last I can look at the world
          quietly and in peace.
I am no longer surprised by the treachery of a friend,
          by the knife concealed in a handshake.
It is useless—the enemy cannot provoke me now.
I passed through the forest of idols
          with my axe—
          how easily they all came down.
I put the things I believed in to the test once more,
     I'm thankful that most of them turned out pure.
I have never been radiant this way,
               never free like this.
The last dark is dawning for me.
At last I can look at the world
          quietly and in peace.
It suddenly comes upon me out of the past
when I'm not looking—
          a word
               a smell
                    the gesture of a hand.
                    The word is friendly
                         the smell beautiful,
                         the hand is in a hand, my love.
The call of memory no longer makes me sad.
I have no complaints about memories.
In fact, I have no complaints about anything,
not even about my heart
          aching nonstop like a big tooth.

The last dark is dawning for me.
Now neither the pride of the seer nor the scribe's claptrap.
I'm pouring bowls of light over my head,
I can look at the sun and I'm not dazzled.
And perhaps—what a pity—
                the most beautiful lie
                        will no longer seduce me.
Words can't make me drunk any more,
neither mine nor anyone else's.
That's how it goes, my rose.
Death now is awfully close.
The world is a world more beautiful than ever.
The world was my suit of clothes,
                                I started undressing.
I was at the window of a train,
                now I'm at the station.
I was inside the house,
                now I'm at the door—it's open.
I love the guests twice as much.
And the heat is blonder than ever,
                        the snow is whiter than ever.

21 July 1957

Soon after you left
it got cold and snowed.
When that happens they say
the sky cried for the dead.
But you know, that's spring.
On the 13th of April the sun opened up.
Prague suddenly smiled
even there, at the cemetery.
Though they still speak of you
almost as if they were praying,
your black-veiled photo
stands bright and sunny in the shop window.
The weather might turn bad again,
but then we're facing May . . .
May in Prague, you know
green, gold-yellow.
When it attacks the streets
young girls wipe grief
like window panes
and the grief you left us
will vanish like your shadow
from the sidewalks of Prague.
This world . . . But to tell the truth,
life-loving, smart,
the good-hearted dead
don't want forty days of mourning
nor do they say "After me the deluge!"
Leaving behind some helpful things, a few words,
a tree, a smile,
each gets up and goes
and does not share with the living
the darkness of the tomb
and carries by himself
the weight of his stone.
And because they want nothing from
the living,
it's as if they aren't dead . . .

I know you too Nezval
are like this,
you too are one of the good-hearted,
world-loving, smart
dead of Prague.

to Ekber Babayev

The snow is knee-deep in the courtyard
and still coming down hard—
it hasn't let up all morning.
We're in the kitchen.
On the table, on the oilcloth, spring,
on the table, there's a very tender young cucumber
                pebbly, and fresh as a daisy.
We're sitting around the table looking at it.
It softly lights up our faces,
and the very air smells fresh.
We're sitting around the table looking at it,
amazed
       thoughtful
              optimistic.
We're as if in a dream.
On the table, on the oilcloth, hope,
on the table, beautiful days
a cloud seeded with a green sun
an emerald crowd impatient and on the way
loves blooming openly
on the table, there on the oilcloth, a very tender young
                              cucumber
                  pebbly, and fresh as a daisy.
The snow is knee-deep in the courtyard
and coming down hard.
It hasn't let up all morning.

March 1960 Moscow

The chairs are asleep on their feet
                    the same as the table
the rug lies stretched out on its back
                    clenching its embroidery
the mirror is sleeping
the eyes of the windows are closed very tight
the balcony sleeps dangling its legs over the edge
on the opposite roof the chimneys are sleeping
                    the same as the acacias on the sidewalk
the cloud is sleeping
          with a star on its chest
the light's asleep indoors and out
you woke up my rose
the chairs woke up
      and scrambled from corner to corner
                    the same as the table
the rug sat up straight
                slowly unfolding its design
like a lake at sunrise the mirror awakened
the windows opened their big blue eyes
the balcony woke up
          and pulled its legs out of the air
on the opposite roof the chimneys smoked
the acacias on the sidewalk broke into song
the cloud woke up
          and tossed the star on its chest into our room
the light woke up indoors and out
                    flooding your hair
                          it slipped through your fingers
      and embraced your naked waist those white feet of yours.

May 1960 Moscow

I was born in 1902
I never once went back to my birthplace
I don't like to turn back
at three I served as a pasha's grandson in Aleppo
at nineteen as a student at Moscow Communist University
at forty-nine I was back in Moscow as a guest of the Tcheka
                                                        Party
and I've been a poet since I was fourteen
some people know all about plants some about fish
                                        I know separation
some people know the names of the stars by heart
                                        I recite absences
I've slept in prisons and in grand hotels
I've known hunger even a hunger strike and there's almost no
                                        food I haven't tasted
at thirty they wanted to hang me
at forty-eight to give me the Peace Medal
                                                which they did
at thirty-six I covered four square meters of concrete in
                                                half a year
at fifty-nine I flew from Prague to Havana in eighteen hours
I never saw Lenin I stood watch at his coffin in '24
in '61 the tomb that I visit is his books
they tried to tear me away from my party
                                        it didn't work
nor was I crushed under falling idols
in '51 I sailed with a young friend into the teeth of death
in '52 I spent four months flat on my back with a broken
                                        heart waiting for death
I was jealous of the women I loved
I didn't envy Charlie Chaplin one bit
I deceived my women
I never talked behind my friends' backs
I drank but not every day
I earned my bread money honestly what happiness

out of embarrassment for another I lied
I lied so as not to hurt someone else
                    but I also lied for no reason at all
I've ridden in trains planes and cars
most people don't get the chance
I went to the opera
                    most people can't go they haven't even heard of
                                                        the opera
and since '21 I haven't been to the places that most people
                                                        visit
                    mosques churches temples synagogues sorcerers
                    but I've had my coffee grounds read
my writings are published in thirty forty languages
                    in my Turkey in my Turkish they're banned
cancer hasn't caught up with me yet
and nothing says that it has to
I'll never be a prime minister or anything like that
and I'm not interested in such a life
nor did I go to war
or burrow in bomb shelters in the bottom of the night
and I never had to take to the roads under diving planes
but I fell in love at close to sixty
in short comrades
even if today in Berlin I'm *croaking* of grief
                    I can say that I've lived like a human being
and who knows
                    how much longer I'll live
                        what else will happen to me.

This autobiography was written in East Berlin
on September 11th in the year 1961.

I STEPPED OUT OF MY THOUGHTS OF DEATH

I stepped out of my thoughts of death
and put on the June leaves of the boulevards
those of May after all were too young for me
a whole summer is waiting for me a city summer with its hot
                                        stones and asphalt
with its ice-cold pop ice cream sweaty movie houses thick-
                                voiced actors from the provinces
with its taxis that disappear suddenly on big football days
and with its trees that turn to paper under the lights of
                                the Hermitage garden
and maybe with Mexican songs or Ghana tom-toms
and with the poems that I'm going to read on the balcony
and with your hair cut a little shorter
a city summer is waiting for me
I put on the June leaves of the boulevards
I stepped out of my thoughts of death

24 May 1962

it's 1962 March 28th
I'm sitting by the window on the Prague-Berlin train
night is falling
I never knew I liked
night descending like a tired bird on the smoky wet plain
I don't like
likening the descent of evening to that of a tired bird

I didn't know I loved the soil
can someone who hasn't worked the soil love it
I've never worked the soil
it must be my only Platonic love

and here I've loved the river all this time
whether motionless like this it curls skirting the hills
European hills topped off with chateaus
or whether it stretches out flat as far as the eye can see
I know you can't wash in the same river even once
I know the river will bring new lights that you will not see
I know we live slightly longer than a horse and not nearly
                                        as long as a crow
I know this has troubled people before
                        and will trouble those after me
I know all this has been said a thousand times before
                        and will be said after me

I didn't know I liked the sky
cloudy or clear
the blue vault that Andrei watched on his back on the
                                battlefield at Borodino
in prison I translated both volumes of *War and Peace* into
                                Turkish
I hear voices
not from the blue vault but from the yard
the guards are beating someone again

I didn't know I loved trees
bare beeches around Moscow in Peredelkino
they come upon me in winter noble and modest
beeches are counted as Russian the way we count poplars as
                                            Turkish

"the poplars of Izmir
losing their leaves . . .
they call us The Knife—
                        lover like a young tree . . .
we blow stately mansions sky-high"
Ilgaz forest, 1920: I tied a linen handkerchief edged with
                            embroidery to a pine bough

I never knew I loved roads
even the asphalt kind
Vera's behind the wheel we're driving from Moscow to the
                                            Crimea
                                    Koktebele
                    formerly "Göktepe ili" in Turkish
the two of us inside a closed box
the world flows past on both sides distant and mute
I was never this close to anyone in my life
bandits came upon me on the red road between Bolu and
                            Gerede and I am eighteen
apart from my life I don't have anything in the wagon that
                                        they can take
and at eighteen our lives are what we value least
I've written this somewhere before
wading through the dark muddy street I'm going to the
                                            Karagöz
Ramazan night
the paper lantern leading the way
maybe nothing like this ever happened
maybe I read it somewhere an eight-year-old boy going to the
                                        shadow play
Ramazan night in Istanbul holding his grandfather's hand
        his grandfather has on a fez and is wearing the fur coat
            with the sable collar over his robe
        and there's a lantern in the servant's hand

and I can't contain myself for joy
flowers come to mind for some reason
poppies cactuses jonquils
in the jonquil garden in Kadiköy Istanbul I kissed Marika
fresh almonds on her breath
I'm seventeen
my heart on a swing touched the sky
I didn't know I loved flowers
friends sent me three red carnations in prison
I just remembered the stars
I love them too
whether I'm floored watching them from below
or whether I'm flying by their side

I have some questions for the cosmonauts
did they see the stars much larger
were they like huge jewels on black velvet
                              or apricots on orange
does it make a person feel proud to get a little closer
                                        to the stars
I saw color photos of the cosmos in Ogonek magazine
now don't get upset friends but nonfigurative shall we say or
abstract well some of them looked just like such paintings
which is to say they were terribly figurative and concrete
my heart was in my mouth looking at them
they are the endlessness of our longing to grasp things
looking at them I could think even of death and not feel one
                                        bit sad
I never knew I loved the cosmos

snow flashes in front of my eyes
both heavy wet steady snow and the dry whirling kind
I didn't know I liked snow
I never knew I loved the sun
even when setting cherry-red as now
in Istanbul too it sometimes sets in postcard colors
but you aren't about to paint it like that

I didn't know I loved the sea
                              or how much
—putting aside the Sea of Azov

I didn't know I loved the clouds
whether I'm under or up above them
whether they look like giants or shaggy white beasts

moonlight the most false the most languid the most petit-
                                        bourgeois
strikes me
I like it
I didn't know I liked rain
whether it falls like a fine net or splatters against the glass
my heart leaves me tangled up in a net or trapped inside a drop
and takes off for uncharted countries I didn't know I loved
rain but why did I suddenly discover all these passions sitting
by the window on the Prague-Berlin train
is it because I lit my sixth cigarette
one alone is enough to kill me
is it because I'm almost dead from thinking about someone
                                        back in Moscow
her hair straw-blond eyelashes blue

the train plunges on through the pitch-black night
I never knew I liked the night pitch-black
sparks fly from the engine
I didn't know I loved sparks
I didn't know I loved so many things and I had to wait until I
was sixty to find it out sitting by the window on the Prague-
Berlin train watching the world disappear as if on a journey
from which one does not return

19 April 1962 Moscow

Page 5: **A Spring Writing Left in the Middle:** Babiâli is the street in Istanbul where all the publishing houses are located.

Page 11: **Gioconda and Si-Ya-U:** "Si-ya-u" is Hsiao San, Chinese revolutionary and man of letters. Born in 1896 and one of the thirteen original members of Mao's New People's Study Society, he was a high-ranking member of the Chinese Communist Party's committees on literature and culture throughout the fifties and early sixties. Hikmet met him when they were both students in Moscow in the early twenties, and he wrote this poem believing that Hsiao had been executed in Shanghai after returning to China. Hikmet found out afterwards that his friend was still alive, and they met in Vienna in 1951 and traveled to Peking together in 1952. This poem was translated into Chinese, but it was later burned—along with Hsiao's books—in the Cultural Revolution. Hikmet, who conceived of the poem as a verse-novel, freely mixes fact with fiction; for example, just as Shanghai was in fact the scene of one of the bloodiest crackdowns on Chinese Communists during the twenties, La Gioconda actually disappeared from the Louvre in May of 1924, and Hsiao *was* in Paris before going to Moscow to study. This conversion of facts into a decidedly fictional whole, together with the radical transformation of art into life *within* the poem, serves ultimately to break down the distinction between art and life.

Page 39: **They:** This is the prologue to Hikmet's *Epic of the Independence War*, written in 1939–41.

Page 44: **26 September 1945:** This and the following poem are from the sequence *Poems Written Between 9 and 10 PM*, which Hikmet wrote for his second wife Piraye.

Page 64: **Letter from Istanbul:** Münevver Andaç was Hikmet's third wife; the Turkish government prevented her from joining him in exile. Educated in France, she has translated some of his work into French.

Page 73: **Conversation with Dead Nezval:** Vítězslav Nezval (1900–58), Czech poet.

Page 75: **The Cucumber:** Ekber Babayev was Hikmet's friend throughout the thirteen years of his exile and is the editor of his *Complete Works*, which began to appear in Sofia in 1967.

Page 76: **Vera Waking from Sleep:** Vera Tulyakova, the young woman Hikmet lived with during the last years of his life.